# *Bilingual Blues*

*(Poems, 1981-1994)*

Gustavo Pérez Firmat

Bilingual Press/Editorial Bilingüe
TEMPE, ARIZONA

© 1995 by Bilingual Press/Editorial Bilingüe

ISBN  0-927534-47-9

**Library of Congress Cataloging-in-Publication Data**

Pérez Firmat, Gustavo, 1949-
    Bilingual blues: poems, 1981-1994 / by Gustavo Pérez Firmat.
        p.    cm.
    Poems in English and Spanish.
    ISBN  0-927534-47-9
    1. Cuban Americans—Poetry.    I. Title.
PS3566.E69138B55  1994
811' .54—dc20                    94-32331
                                            CIP

*Cover design by Kerry Curtis*

*Cover art by James Rivera Carey*

*Back cover photo by Mary Anne Pérez*

**Acknowledgments**

Funding provided by a grant from the National Endowment for the Arts in Washington, D.C., a Federal agency.

Major new marketing initiatives have been made possible by the Lila Wallace-Reader's Digest Literary Publishers Marketing Development Program, funded through a grant to the Council of Literary Magazines and Presses.

"Lime Cure," "On Whether My Father Deserves a Poem," "Evita y Gustavito," "Quiet Time," "The Poet's Mother Gives Him a Birthday Present," "What's Wrong With Me," and "The Operation" are reprinted with permission from the publisher of *The Americas Review* Vol. 20, No. 1 (Houston: Arte Público Press-University of Houston, 1992).

*Acknowledgments continue on p. 128.*

# Bilingual Blues

# Bilingual Press/Editorial Bilingüe

General Editor
   Gary D. Keller

Managing Editor
   Karen S. Van Hooft

Associate Editors
   Ann Waggoner Aken
   Theresa Hannon

Assistant Editor
   Linda St. George Thurston

Editorial Board
   Juan Goytisolo
   Francisco Jiménez
   Eduardo Rivera
   Mario Vargas Llosa

Address:
Bilingual Review/Press
Hispanic Research Center
Arizona State University
Box 872702
Tempe, Arizona 85287-2702
(602) 965-3867

# Contents

*For Miriam,*
*witty and wise*

# 1

*Justified Margins*

# DEDICATION

The fact that I
am writing to you
in English
already falsifies what I
wanted to tell you.
My subject:
how to explain to you
that I
don't belong to English
though I belong nowhere else,
if not here
in English.

# SEEING SNOW

Had my father, my grandfather, and his,
had they been asked whether I would ever see snow,
they certainly—in another language—
would have answered,
no. Seeing snow for me
will always mean a slight or not so slight
suspension of the laws of nature.
I was not born to see snow.
I was not meant to see snow.
Even now, snowbound as I've been
all these years,
my surprise does not subside.
What, exactly, am I doing here?
Whose house is this, anyway?
For sure one of us has strayed.
For sure someone's lost his way.
This must not be the place.
Where I come from, you know,
it's never snowed:
not once, not ever, not yet.

# CHAPEL HILL

Here
we hold our breath
until we're blue
(Carolina blue).
There
we breathe fast
and deep.
Divers in reverse,
we go down for air.
Our lives transpire asth-
matically, by pants and heaves:
chronic asphyxia relieved
by holidays of respiration.

# BEFORE I WAS A WRITER

I used to go
to the Little Professor Bookstore
and leaf through southern novels by
Smith or Price or Rubin
and wish I had my own.

*El son y la furia*:
a bold, breathtaking fictional exploration
of Carolina Cubanness,
the first part set in La Loma del Chaple,
the second in Chapel Hill
(sometimes things translate),
recounting the life and opinions of one—or
several—Gustavo Francisco Tomás Pérez Firmat
from adolescence to adulthood to battered senility at thirty-two.

But that was before I was a writer.
Now I'm happy
just to think
that tomorrow or the day after
we'll be riding
that same umbilical interstate,
that same life-support highway system,
that same taut arm reaching
back to Miami, mi mami.

# LIMEN

We took David back up just when
he was beginning to learn to speak,
to say agua and mamá and galletica.
(Miami es mar y calor y comida.)
Just when he was on the threshold,
at the limen,
perinatal to his past, to me,
we delivered him to y'alls and drawls,
to some place I've never lived in all these years
I've been living there.
(My words are also agua and mamá and galletica
and a few improper names like El Farito,
Chirino, and Dadeland, which is not English
now, though it used to be.)
Just as David was beginning to say
the language I breathe in,
we moved him up and inland away
from warmth and water,
knotting his tongue—my tongue—with distance.

# WORDS FOR A SOUTHERN SONG

Ain't got no mother
tongue.
Ain't got no father
land.
Jes had some black-eyed
peas.
Jes had some country
ham.

I'm jest a Southern
boy.
I'm jest a country
man.
I keep my belly
full.
And do the best I
can.

Ain't got no mother
tongue.
Ain't got no father
land.
Jes had some black-eyed
peas.
Jes had some country
ham.

# CAROLINA BLUES

Everything here is blue.
I've got a blue streak a mile wide
and it won't wash off.
I've complained about it till I'm blue in the face.
I'm seeing blue.
Blue grass in Kentucky is contra natura:
it belongs right here in Carolina.

I hate blue movies, blue boys, blue babies.
To hell with my blue heaven, I don't wanna go.
Vida Blue is my least favorite pitcher
and Bill Blue my least favorite critic.
If you find a true-blue friend, lose him.
I'm not sure what a bluenose is, but I don't like it.
If God is a tarheel,
he'd have chosen another color.

Give me tritanopia (look it up).
Give me autumn, killer of blues.
Oh for grey skies, yellow leaves, hazel eyes,
black hair, red bricks, white houses.
Oh for all things beautiful and unblue.
Oh for another shot at the spectrum.

9

# AFTERPOEM TO "GIRL IN A BIKINI"

I would recant that poem, if I could,
except I never throw out text.
The poem makes me feel a little guilty.
It might be read as sexist.
My wife will not enjoy it.
No one will publish it.

Am I really a pig after all?
And what would poemed nymph opine?

But my poem is so small it fits
inside her bikini. Is so slight
she could swallow it in one gulp.
Is so tiny she'd take it in at a glance
and never feel a thing.

# ON HAPPINESS / UNHAPPINESS

### I

Nobody's happy anymore.
I'm not happy.
You're not happy.
Even Sarah's not happy
although she lives in Boston
and is pregnant for the second time.
It may be that happiness is no longer
a relevant category of experience.
It may be that we should stop asking the question.
It may be that we should stop using the word.

### II

Not even the citizens of heaven
are in heaven all the time.
They come down for coffee.
They go to the bathroom.
They take a break from ecstasy,
strung out from so much beatific vision.
The elect have problems too, you know.
Not even the citizens of heaven
are in heaven all the time.

### III

I can no longer write as I once never did.
I am no longer the man I never was.
My life knows no degree:
no cooling, no slipping, no loss of pitch.
I transpire on one dull level with one dull ache.
I will never be one day older than I am now,
or ever was.

## IV

Not here: I know,
weary. But where?
Not here: I know,
dreary. Who cares
is there: I know.
All there, I know.
If anywhere.

# MAD FOR MUSH

No such thing as too much mush.
My life, mi vida, es mush.
You, mi vida, eres too mush.
Mientras más mucho mejor.

Mad for mush.
Made for mush.
Dame más.
Dame mash.
Dame mush.

## MY STRUGGLE

To call Rosa,
say Mrs. Pérez, please,
and not be met
with, what was that, sir?
—and then, silence.
I've made mighty efforts not to mumble.
Imagine, I used to say,
May I speak with Professor Pérez, please.
Now I only try
that on days I've had a brilliant idea
or an article accepted.

## BACON

Let them have motion.
Let them be sensitive.
Leave to them depth of feeling,
subtlety of understanding,
complicated loves.

I'm square
on the side of inarticulate glee.

For me the melody of dishwashers.
For me the mortal grave,
the housefuls, the can of beer,
bacon.

For me the things
that never leave a thing.

# SOMETIMES ALL YOU WANT

Sometimes all you want
is the peacefulness of Wednesday nights,
our sofa,
the door half open to hear
the night and exorcise my holy smoke.

No roads or inroads
no ventures or adventures
content with my limitation,
my occasional Armani tie
and Miami.

Sometimes not enough
is good enough.
Sometimes not enough
is all you could ever want.

# LAS NAVIDADES DEL 10 DE OCTUBRE

I woke up this morning thinking
it was Christmas day,
mistaking David's tinkering
for toys.

Outside the small pines seemed
incomplete
in their greenness, seemed
colorless where they sat.

The explanation is obvious, even prosaic: anytime the
thermometer dips below 65 and the sky is sunny and cloudless,
my body forgets that I no longer live someplace where bright,
cool mornings betoken anything other than autumn.

# WAITING GAME

A Cuban has holed himself
up in a sleeping car in Raleigh, North Carolina.
He has been there since Friday and
today it is Sunday.
He has shot and killed his wife.
His daughter, who is nine months old, has dehydrated.
His son, who is four, occupies the hours
asking his mother to wake up.

One Cuban of uncertain origins and destination
has locked himself up
in a sleeping car in a sleeping city
and the swat teams lie in wait.
They wait:
for the son to stop talking
for the father to start shooting
for the dead to start rotting
for the crisis to resolve itself
peacefully and without incident.

# NATIVES LIKE US

The annual 4th of July party
in Carrboro and everybody here's
natives like us.

The Southern Dreamers play Hank Williams.
David goes for Coke and gets lost,
I find him crying in a sea of rednecks.
Shoeless, but not quite American,
happy, but not quite at home,
Miriam dives into the sandbox.
We buy everything in sight.

Then it's fireworks
and all the natives like us
cheer the feast of lights.
(Even the Vietnamese look up.)
It's over, we begin to leave.
David complains, Miriam complains.
I think: this half-life is whole-life,
and promise next year we'll go to the movies.

## SUMMER NIGHTS

When our children grow up
in North Carolina
who will they be?
It's not so easy, Rosa,
everything has consequences,
gives you something to think about
on summer nights.
Where's the city, the hub, the conversations?
Why should we trade passion for pastoral
when neither one of us was born on a farm?
It's not so easy, Rosa,
everything has consequences,
gives you something to think about
on summer nights.

# SON/SONG

Sometimes I get
the fee
ling that eve
ry word I writ
e deserves a li
ne to itself.
So cha, so cha, so cha
cha
cha
rged with me
aning, with son
g, do they see
m.

# HOME

Give a guy a break.
Take him back, let him step
on soil that's his or feels his,
let him have a tongue,
a story, a geography.
Let him not trip back and forth between
bilingualisms,
hyphens,
explanations.
As it is he's a walking-talking bicameral page.
Two hemispheres and neither one likes the other.
Ambidextrous.
Omnipossibilist.
Multivocal.
Let him stop having to translate himself
to himself
endlessly.
Give the guy a break:
crease him, slip him into an envelope,
address it, and let him go.
Home.

# SON-SEQUENCE

Call these poems a son-sequence:
Son as plural being.
Son as rumba beat.
Son as progeny.
Son, fueron, serán.
Son, danzón, guaracha.
Son, his father's son.
Is he?

# CAROLINA CUBAN

Carolina Cuban I'd always thought
was to be a book or poem about me.
But tonight
in the OB section of
Memorial Hospital,
after fifteen hours of Rosa's labor,
two shots of Demerol,
the epidural and several valiums,
I know that Carolina Cuban
will be you, David or Miriam.

You will be the true tarheel cubiche,
the real mixed thing.
(I'm not mixed, just mixed up.)
But you will be a rare
Carolina blue plate of
        lechón con grits;
        iced tea and tasajo:
coño, with a southern drawl.

You, Miriam or David,
first of la raza cósmica,
right here in Chapel Hill, North Carolina,
on June 10, 1981,
at one o'clock in the morning.

# A LIKELY STORY

Digging for roots in his grandmother's yard
between Little Havana and Coral Gables
(we're speaking English today)
David found two toy soldiers, green in their prime,
one kneeling with a bazooka,
the other on his platform-feet aiming a gun
that wasn't there.

The story is this:
I brought them from Cuba in 1960.
Some time later (not too long,
since I gave up soldiering at 12),
I lost them in the yard.
In the 1970s, Shotzie, our dog then
(now nothing), buried them in his pen.
And today (February 1987, dog and pen long passé)
David, accompanied by his grandmother
(whose story this is), finds them while digging for roots
between Little Havana and Coral Gables.

# TURNING THE TIMES TABLES

*I am the sum total of my language.*
*—Charles Sanders Peirce*

¿Y si soy más de uno, Peirce?
¿Y si soy dos,
o tres
o—como diría David—
un millón?
¿En qué momento, en qué participio del mundo
se convierte tu suma en mi resta, Peirce?

I am what is left
after the subtraction of my languages.
I am the division that resists
the multiplication of my languages.
I am the number that won't square,
the figure you can't figure,
the remainder of my languages.

One into two
won't go.
You into tú
won't go.
You into yo
won't go.
I into yo
won't go.
Nothing into nada
won't go.

Split the difference.
Split the atom.
Split.
I still won't go.

Some people
just
don't add
up.

# BILINGUAL BLUES

Soy un ajiaco de contradicciones.
I have mixed feelings about everything.
Name your tema, I'll hedge;
name your cerca, I'll straddle it
like a cubano.

I have mixed feelings about everything.
Soy un ajiaco de contradicciones.
Vexed, hexed, complexed,
hyphenated, oxygenated, illegally alienated,
psycho soy, cantando voy:
You say tomato,
I say tu madre;
You say potato,
I say Pototo.
Let's call the hole
un hueco, the thing
a cosa, and if the cosa goes into the hueco,
consider yourself en casa,
consider yourself part of the family.

Soy un ajiaco de contradicciones,
un puré de impurezas:
a little square from Rubik's Cuba
que nadie nunca acoplará.
(Cha-cha-chá.)

## MUMBLE KING

I am most me when I mumble.
A native mumbler of two languages,
I have mastered the art of imprecision
and of indecision, haltingly.

No me podrán quitar mi dolorido sentir,
this little pain in my corazoncito
that makes me stutter
barbarismos y barbaridades.

Por example:
el cubano-americano es un estar que no sabe dónde es.
Por example:
el cubano-americano se nutre de lo que le falta.

Cubano-americano: ¿dónde soy?
Soy la marca entre un no y un am:
filósofo del no
filósofo del ah, no
filósofo del anón
(que seguramente nunca habré probado).

Cubano-americano: ¿dónde soy?
son que se fue de Cuba
corazón que dejé enterrado
rinconcito de mi tierra
pedacito de cielo: ¿dónde soy?
Un extraviado
Un faccioso
Un inconforme
Un dividido
cuba: no
america: no
¿Dónde soy?
Sólo sé que nadar sé.
Sólo sé que tengo sed.

Dame un trago.
Dame un break.
Dame un besito en el—ah, no—
y hazme olvidar mis penas.

# NOBODY KNOWS MY NAME

I'm tired
dead anonymous tired
of getting mail addressed
to all those people I never was:

| | |
|---|---|
| Gustazo | Peres |
| Gustavio | Penley |
| Gary | Porris |
| Gus | Perry |
| Gustaf | Pirey. |

Nobody here knows my name.
This would never have happened in Havana.

## INTER-STATE

An I
for an I
for an I-95.

# 2

*Equivocaciones*

# A MI HERMANO EL IMPOSTOR

Fuiste tanto yo, que casi no me conozco.
Fuiste el nombre y el hombre.
Fuiste mis números, todos.
Fuiste profesor y propietario
(todo lo mío fue tuyo, no es un decir).
De las confusiones onomásticas de mamá
hiciste dilemas existenciales.

Por ti, mi vida fue otra.
Por ti, me persiguen banqueros y telefonistas.
Por ti, tiemblo ligeramente al firmar Gustavo.

Con todo (y ha sido mucho)
¿quién soy yo para despreciarte?
Una leve permutación genética
y hubiéramos trocado papeles:
yo, el impostor; tú, el impostado.
Además—y aquí va lo importante—
nunca fuimos tan hermanos
tan carne de la misma carne
como cuando tú, con un ligero temblor,
también firmabas Gustavo.

# CARNET DE IDENTIDAD

Hoy jueves veintinueve de marzo
a las siete menos cuarto de la noche
David—espontáneamente—
descubrió la trompetilla:
confirmada su precaria cubanía.

Palmas contra carrillos
(siempre es cuestión de palmas),
un disparo de sus pequeños si potentes pulmones
(siempre los mismos vientos)
bastó para concitar
el huracán en una boca.

Cute, percute y repercute la trompetilla
histórica en todo el estado,
desde las montañas hasta el mar:
trompetillazo a lo tarheel,
bandera sonora de una patria
sin más lugar que mi poema.

# DIA DE LOS PADRES EN CHAPEL HILL

Hoy celebro mi enajenación
multiplicada por dos.
Hoy celebro esos extraños, mis hijos,
en quienes no me reproduzco.
Celebro todo lo que no soy yo
y me rodea
todo lo que soy yo
y me falta.

También celebro la geografía de mi cerebro
escindido en hemisferios,
mi corazón ventrílocuo y mis lenguas.
Celebro, en fin, lo de siempre:
     mi ansia de mar
     mi sed de arena
     mi tristeza tropical
     la latitud y longitud de mis poemas.

## ELEGIAS MINIMAS

### I

Morirse de cáncer
en el exilio
es ser invadido y conquistado
por la sustancia misma de la separación.

El cuerpo extraño–foreign body–
nos corroe con su extranjeridad.
Cada célula maligna se aloja
en el útero o en un pulmón
como un pedacito de alguien que no soy yo,
alguien que habla en inglés
y detesta el café con leche
y a cuyas costumbres
irremisiblemente
terminaré por convertirme.

### II

Ha muerto Norman Barlow:
no lo conocí.

Durante seis años nos cruzamos a diario
sin proferir palabra ni saludo:
fuimos como hermanos.

Nunca existió para mí,
ya no existe para nadie.

Descanse en paz pero sin júbilo
Norman Barlow, cero humano.

### III

Ya no seremos lo que nunca fuimos
y mucho me remuerde, Isabel.
Para la próxima vez
Para la próxima vez
Para la próxima vez te doy mi palabra

(y es lo mejor que tengo)
que no apago tus entusiasmos
que no descuelgo el teléfono
que no dejo que me dejes en paz.

IV

Ha pedido que lo entierren
con un Partagás en la boca.
Sin hábito, sin hálito, sin humo:
ceniza con la ceniza.

# ENTRE HERMANOS

Hermano, yo a ti no te conozco
y tú a mí no me leerás.
Nos separan tu indiferencia y mi cansancio
(o tu cansancio y mi indiferencia, da igual).
Nos separan tus palabras y mis pausas,
tus júbilos y mis vacilaciones.
La cotidianidad, que debiera unirnos,
nos separa también:
tantos años de convivencia sin confluencia.
Porque aquí, entre hermanos,
no existe ni siquiera un camino,
ningún tránsito compartido, ningún sendero por compartir.
Aquí, entre hermanos,
nadie nunca ha dicho nada a nadie.
Aquí, sencillamente, no ha pasado nada.
Por eso te digo ahora, hermano que no escuchas
(hermano que no existes),
que yo a ti no te conozco
y que tú a mí no me leerás.

# OYE BROTHER

Oye brother. Tú eres mi hermano, claro.
Tú eres mi sangre, claro.
No te olvidé, claro.
Pero son veinte años,
pero ya es otro mundo,
pero somos distintos, claro,
aunque somos iguales.

Oye brother. Tú eres mi tierra, claro,
pero mucho ha cambiado,
aunque tú eres my brother, claro,
aunque somos cubanos.

Pero. Claro. Aunque.
Aunque. Pero. Claro.

Miami, verano de 1980

# EXAMEN DE FAMILIA

Hoy quiero poner en limpio algunas cosas
para después borrarlas para siempre.

Tú eres mejor que tu estirpe
y no hace falta hablar de la mía.
La familia es una fatalidad
que se cura con los años, y en nosotros
el tratamiento va bastante adelantado.
Tú y yo nacimos para semilla o tronco,
no para rama o follaje y mucho menos
(a pesar de tu nombre) para flor:
sean otros orgullo y ornamento
de nuestras respetables familias.

Hay que decirlo: en los momentos cruciales
la familia exige pero no acompaña.
Mas no desesperes:
hace rato ya que nuestras sangres dispersas
se han trocado en savia y sabiduría,
en una sangre sola.
Amame a mí, que soy tu prójimo,
nunca tendrás más padre o madre o hermano o hermana
que yo.

## MI CASA

Esta casa ya no es mía,
no la rigen mis fantasmas:
otros íncubos ocupan el ámbito familiar.

Me busco en las sombras de los pasillos
y no me encuentro.
Me busco en las caras de las paredes
y no me encuentro.
Me busco en el espejo del baño memorable
y no me encuentro.
Hasta el zumbido de las habitaciones
me dice que no estoy.

# VIVIR EN FANTASMAS

Hay familias firmes y finales,
fijas en la memoria y en las fotografías.
Hay otras familias—menos firmes,
más finales—tejidas de fantasmas:
así la tuya y la mía.

Pongo por caso: mi tío Pepe, sordo y sifilítico,
siempre en broma, con su sufrida Josefina:
fantasma de la alegría.
Pongo por caso: la abuelita que no viste
y te mece en el recuerdo:
fantasma de tu otra vida.

Una noche como hoy, que me siento
triste y despoblado, ellos me habitan.
Los invoco uno a uno—
Pepe, Octavio, Manolo, Ricardo—
cada cual puntual y necesario,
cada cual animado por algo que no será el recuerdo,
será ansia, ganas de vivir,
codicia de futuro suya y mía.

Y esa ansia va cobrando cuerpo,
dibuja una faz, unas figuras
que se parecen un tanto a mí
mas no me pertenecen.
Y al cabo de la noche,
ya rodeado de seres y siluetas,
ya en familia de fantasmas
me siento más yo:
no creador sino creado.

Hacen falta los fantasmas
más vivos que muchos vivos.
Hacen falta los fantasmas
más vivos nosotros por ellos.

# DOS ALAS ENORMES Y BLANCAS

Tengo a un hermano en la cárcel
y a un hijo enfermo.
O a un hijo en prisión
y a un hermano agonizante.
Tengo dos alas enormes y blancas,
me pesan como una genealogía.
Dos alas, una sobre cada hombro,
una sobre cada hombre de los que soy
y no puedo despegarlas.

Es un pegote de alas, una plasta de plumas
y cartílagos sobre mis hombros
y no puedo despegarlas.

Qué no daría por dormir sin alas
(estoy dispuesto a sacrificar los hombros)
Qué no daría por dormir sin alas
(estoy dispuesto a sacrificar la estirpe)
Qué no daría por dormir sin alas.

## POEMA DE LA CENIZA

Me pides que recuerde mi casa
(ésa donde me crié): no puedo hacerlo.
Mi casa eres tú, y los niños,
pues ya no presumo de otro hogar que el nuestro.

Si alguna vez tuve padre: ceniza.
Si alguna vez tuve madre: ceniza.
Lo que fue ombligo: ceniza.
Lo que fue matriz: ceniza.
Todo mi pasado vinculante: ceniza.
Sopla una brisa del sur y fulgura algún rescoldo:
    ceniza, ceniza.
Ochocientas treinta y tres millas de ceniza.
Treinta y seis años de ceniza.
Dos libros y este poema, ceniza.

Ceniza soy
(sin fénix).

# VIVIR SIN HISTORIA

He viajado poco, he vivido menos.
No se explica este cansancio y sin embargo
estoy cansado.

Desde mi margen contemplo
a los hombres-pararrayos, a los hombres-volcán,
a los hombres-liebre.
Contemplo al héroe de última hora
y al mártir del momento.
Contemplo las inmolaciones, los sacrificios,
las bellas catástrofes que harán historia.

Yo no tengo historia
y sin embargo estoy cansado.

Cansado de la historia, entre otras cosas,
y de las inmolaciones
y de los sacrificios
y de las bellas catástrofes
y sobre todo de los héroes
y sobre todo de los mártires.

Pudrirse de grima en una cárcel
puede ser mala suerte o mala leche.
Mas ya cansa tanta tragedia:
tanta viuda atrincherada en su luto,
tanto hijo huérfano,
tanto exilio, tanto padecer.

La orfandad es bonita pero también cansa.
El dolor de los demás es bonito pero también cansa.
Atención bayameses:
bajad las voces
detened la marcha

deponed las banderas
y las bayonetas.

Traigo un secreto que confiaros:
vivir sin historia es vivir.

# EN MIAMI
## (DESCARGA)

Miami es mucha bulla y poca ebullición.
Miami es muchas caras y más caricaturas.
Miami es un cohete cargado de futuro.
Miami es un arcabuz cargado de pasado.
(A mí qué me importa que explote Miami.)

Miami es nido, es laberinto,
es agobio es ansiedad es alegría es arrebato.
Miami es mi madre
(y la tuya por si acaso).
En Miami mira que las palabras pesan.
En Miami el mudo es monstruo.
En Miami el sordo cunde.
Miami es una isla de lenguas
rodeada de bla-bla-bla por todas partes.

A mí que me piquen en pedacitos
y me esparzan por la Calle Ocho
entre la 27 y la 12.
A mí que me entierren un huevo en La Esquina de Tejas
y el otro en el condominio de mi suegra.
A mí que me flagelen me torturen me trituren
me saquen los ojos los dientes las uñas
los pezones las pezuñas
todo todo todo todito
pero que sea en Miami.

Miami: mi patria, mi paraíso, mi podredumbre.

# TRES POEMAS MARTIANOS

One

Conozco al monstruo,
he vivido en sus entrañas.
Saben bien.

Two

Conozco al monstruo,
he vivido de sus entrañas.
Yo también soy monstruo.

Three

Conozco al monstruo,
y el monstruo me conoce a mí.
Somos felices en nuestro conocimiento.

# MATRIZ Y MARGEN

*A Roberto Valero*

Roberto: joven hermano mayor
en la poesía y en la historia:
reconozco mi déficit de acontecer.
En tus palabras hay matriz,
en las mías, margen.
En tu acento hay espesor y alarma,
en el mío, reminiscencia.

Y sin embargo reclamo un turno y una voz
en nuestra historia.
Reclamo *marcar* en la cola
de ese ilustre cocodrilo inerte
que nos devora en la distancia.
Reclamo la pertinencia y el mar.

También es matriz mi margen.
Mi recuerdo se espesa como tu acento.
Yo también llevo el cocodrilo a cuestas.
Y digo que sus aletazos verdes me baten
incesantemente.
Y digo que me otorgan la palabra
y el sentido.
Y digo que sin ellos no sería lo que soy
y lo que no soy:
una brisa de ansiedad y recuerdo
soplando hacia otra orilla.

# ELOGIO DE LA INDISCRECION

De todas mis (pocas) virtudes
indiscreción es la que más quiero.
Cultura es cúmulo de indiscreciones
y yo presumo de hombre culto.
De no ser indiscreto, no sería nada.

Discreto el cretino, que no entiende
            el sordo, que no oye
            el mudo, que no sabe hablar.
Yo, que entiendo (un poco), y oigo (bien que mal)
            y hablo (tartamudeo)
me reservo el derecho absoluto a soltar la lengua
            violar confidencias
            publicar intimidades
            provocar escándalos
            y difundir infamias.

Sépase:
no pienso llevarme ni un solo secreto a la tumba.
(Quien busque cómplice en el silencio
que no hable conmigo.)

# FIN DE FIESTA

Sabes que sé cosas que no te digo.
Sé que sabes cosas que no me dices.
Sin embargo: hablamos como nunca.

Mas si lo no dicho tuyo
supera lo no dicho mío,
si lo que tú callas es más
que lo que yo cuento,
ya no hay qué hablar.

Amistad es mentir los dos
lo mismo.

# VOCACIONES

Hoy guardé el Webster
y desempolvé el Sopena.
(De madre)
(De muerte).

O fundo o me fundo.
¡Me fundo!

# PROVOCACIONES

*¿Cómo puede seguir uno viviendo*
*con dos lenguas, dos casas, dos nostalgias*
*dos tentaciones, dos melancolías?*
*–Heberto Padilla, "Postcard to USA"*

Y yo te respondo, Heberto, talmúdicamente:
¿cómo no seguir vivendo con dos
lenguas casas nostalgias tentaciones melancolías?
Porque no puedo amputarme una lengua
ni tumbar una casa
ni enterrar una melancolía.
Quisiera, al contrario,
singularizar lo indivisiblemente dividido,
hacer de dos grandes ojos una sola mirada.

# EQUIVOCACIONES

Soy como el pun, equívoco.
Ofendo.
Caigo mal.
Doy golpes bajos.
Molesto a las señoras
y a las señoritas.

Soy como el pun, equívoco.
Tuerzo el recto sentido.
Habito el hábito de la ambigüedad.
Me ilumina la luz del solecismo.
Suplo mis carencias con ambivalencias.

Soy como el pun:
equivocado de la vida
malcriado de nacimiento
portador de anomie perniciosa
(entre otras y muchas cosas).

Soy el mal acompañante de los mal acompañados.
Soy el bufo, el bofe,
el que llega tarde y se va temprano.
Apesto de lucidez.
Sudo caos.
El decoro que nunca aprendí
ya se me ha olvidado.

## AFORRITMOS

When I hear the word culture I reach for my Gucci.

The best offense is a good Fendi.

No hay mall que por bien no venga.

Il faut cultiver notre Charles Jourdan.

Insanity is not all it's cracked up to be.

Suicide is a dying art.

Discretion is the better part of valium.

If the part is larger than the hole, it won't fit.

Ubi pene, ibi patria.

Coito ergo cum.

I slink therefore I scram.

A menos amor, más turbación.

Home is where my mother hangs her bata.

All roads lead to roam.

Si respiro reviento.

Hysteria repeats itself.

The manía makes the man.

Demons are forever.

Teórico no:  meteórico.

Exilio y socorro.

Tit for twat.

A penis for your thoughts.

Passion is poison.

There's safety in numbness.

Varices is the spice of life.

There's more to egotism than meets the I.

The Last Supper: a fête worse than death.

Via cursi: hombre / hembra / hambre.

Poesía: histeria y estilo.

Poesía: disciplina y desespero.

Poesía: hacer de trips corazón.

Más vale cama que fama.

Cría cama y acuéstate a dormir.

No sólo de puns vive el hombre.

De Gustavo non disputandum est.

Publish or Pérez.

# MEDITACION DEL MAMONCILLO

*para Isabel,*
*melancólica en Shrewsbury*

El mamoncillo es dulce pero amargo. Seduce pero no satisface. Tienta pero no llena. Ya el nombre lo dice: ofrece no el gustazo de un mamón sino el alivio de un mamoncillo. Fruta que frustra, el mamoncillo reduce el placer de mamar, de amar, a su mínima expresión. (Mamar: pesadilla freudiana donde se dan cita mamá, mar, amar. Mi mamá me mama– Edipo dixit, con amargura.) No sé de otra fruta cuyo nombre provenga de la forma de consumo (sin zumo); es como decirle a la manzana "mordida" o al mango "chupada". El mamoncillo es la fruta del árbol de la vida, Isabel; porque en la vida también hemos de contentarnos con itsy-bitsy bites o modestos mamoncillos.

# DÍPTICO DE LA IDENTIDAD

## SOY YOS

# PERVERSO SENCILLO

Yo soy un hombre sin centro
de donde crece la palma.
Y antes de morirme quiero
rayarme una paja en calma.

## FIRMAT DIXIT

Humo sum:
nada cubano
me aliena.
¡puta!

# EXTRAVERSION

A Cuba no es cuestión de visitarla, recordarla, conquistarla o imaginarla. Es cuestión de escribirla. Cuba es una grafía sin geografía, un recurso de mi discurso, una rumba sin rumbo.

## APOLOGIA PRO VITA SUA

Caigo mal
pero
cago bien.

# DESMITIFICACION

Señores:

dejémonos de mitificar
la caca. En fin:
el olor de la caca
el color de la caca
el sabor de la caca:

todo es cuestión
de alimentación.

# CUBANITA DESCUBANIZADA

Cubanita descubanizada
quién te pudiera recubanizar.
Quién supiera devolverte
el ron y la palma,
el alma y el son.

Cubanita descubanizada,
tú que pronuncias todas las eses
y dices ómnibus y autobús,
quién te pudiera
quién te supiera
si te quisieras recubanizar.

# EQUILIBRIO INESTABLE

A una cubana
            en bikini
                        siempre
        le sobra
                o le falta
algo.

## POEMA TÁCITO

Nunca aprendí a hablar.
Soy profesor de pocas palabras
y poeta de pocos poemas.
La parquedad es mi fuerza.

Entre cubanos, donde ser es oírse,
casi no soy:
mi cuchareta es siempre cucharita.

No sé cómo sería yo de niño:
si fabulaba, si inventaba, si contaba historias.
Sé que ahora
callo hasta por los codos.

Y nada más.

# TODO ES TRISTE

*after Virgilio*

Todo es triste.
No hay precaución que baste.
No hay previsión que sirva.

Siempre royendo ruinas.
Siempre bebiendo hueso.

Firme en la aprensión.
Sereno en el desvelo.
Ya se sabe:
todo es triste.

# MIS MANOS

> *Mis manos traen el alba.*
> *–Fayad Jamís*

Mis manos no traen alba
ni mediodía ni crepúsculo
ni medianoche. Mis manos
no traen si no lo que ellas entregan:
un algo de nada en palabras
que dicen mis manos no traen.

# DESCOMPOSICION

Hace tres días que estoy
a sopa clara de pollo (kosher)
claro: y no me repongo (concho)
de esta indigestión ad nauseam.

Mientras tanto sigo queriendo
mi trozo de queso argentino
(courtesy of Southern Season)
la tacita de café
(en mi casa toman Bustelo)
y un puro Partagás
(de Mike's Cigars en la playa).

Pero el dolor de barriga
angst de los intestinos
no me abandona.
Recrudece cuando como,
recrudece cuando escribo,
recrudece frente al televisor:
no hay remedio
(digánselo al médico de los miércoles)
estoy descompuesto para siempre.

# EL MEDICO DE LOS MIERCOLES

El médico de los miércoles
se interesa en mis sueños
y me tilda de psicológico
cuando interpreto los de David
(el oso soy yo).

Habla poco y bajito,
sonríe magnánimamente
como un canguro
y no receta valium.

Impaciente el paciente
me voy con mi salsa para otra parte
donde la neura
cueste menos y rinda más.

## PLANTADO

Digo (me digo) que tanta vuelta
acabará por aplastarnos.
Que no es posible residir (agrio) aquí,
vivir (agrio) allá.
De tanto no ser quien soy
acabaré por no serme.
De tanto no estar donde estoy
acabaré por no estarme.

Mas llegó el momento
de serme y estarme
de llegar y quedarme:
sangre, savia, sabiduría
ahora, en este lugar,
prole, pies y cabeza
definitivamente plantados.

# INMINENCIA DE OTOÑO

Amago o amenaza de óxido en las hojas
de algún árbol junto al lago.
No hay patos, no hay gansos, sobra
el pan y David quiere saber
dónde han ido: le digo que a Miami.

Calla y se acerca a la orilla:
las hojas caen como alas.

# AGUAS MALAS

Todo
lo que no
es mar:
Lagos
Pozos
Pocetas
Piscinas
Cisternas
Charcos
Ríos
Fuentes
Saltos
Geisers
Termas
Lágrimas.

Todo
lo que no
es mar
es agua
mala.

# THE SOUTHERN PART OF HEAVEN

*A César Cauce, muerto por*
*el KKK el tres de noviembre de 1979*
*en una calle de Greensboro, N.C.*

Qué privilegio morir en North Carolina.
De la vida a la muerte, un pasito nada más.
De la muerte a la tumba, otro mínimo pasito.
Y de la tumba al cielo, nada.

Por eso digo que derrumbarse de un tiro
en North Carolina
es caer de cabeza en el cielo.
Y al caer ver a San Pedro esperándote,
en cualquier calle de cualquier pueblo,
con una sábana blanca.

# MI MADRE CUANDO NOS VISITA

Mi madre cuando nos visita
tiñe todo
de familiaridad:
viste de verde y mar
mi jardín de tierra adentro
(cuando ella está mi casa es carabela),
imparte el color del cariño
a estos raros rojos otoñales
y bajo sus pisadas las hojas
crujen amorosamente.

El aire se hace respiración.
La soledad se vuelve habitable.
Lo extraño torna hogareño
cada otoño
cuando nos visita mi madre.

## ROMANCE DE CORAL GABLES

Llego a Miami y es otra claridad,
lucidez verde y transparente:
el patio un oleaje de hojas
que inunda las habitaciones.
Florecen los lladrós
flotan las fotografías
se mecen los tenedores
con este norte que me trae el sur
de la Florida.
El televisor es un barco de velas verdes,
cada lámpara es un mástil:
tallos que retoñan igual que yo,
clorofílico en este mar de vida.

Verde que me quiero verde
(pero mi Granada está en Coral Gables).

# CARNE DE IDENTIDAD

Hoy siento la álgida nostalgia de siempre:
no cambio, no evoluciono, no me acostumbro.
Me he estancado en mi cuerpo,
que tampoco cambia
ni se acostumbra
ni nada.

Soy el que fui, alguna vez, hace años,
para siempre.
Seré el que fui, alguna vez, hace años,
para siempre.
Nazco a mi pasado cotidianamente
sin dejar de parecerme siempre a mí.

Me duplico mas no cambio.
Me propago mas no cambio.
Me arrugo mas no cambio.
Me baño, me afeito, me pelo
mas no cambio.
Me cambio mas no cambio.

No hay remedio: soy quien fui.
No cambio.

# LA LLUVIA

Extraño la lluvia.
Esta noche que por fin llueve a cántaros
sé que la lluvia
ciñe la casa y la protege.
(Por la lluvia volvemos a ser isla.)

Esta noche sé que el auténtico paraíso
no fue el jardín sino el arca:
Noé con vástagos y criaturas
dormidos entre tablas:
piel con piel, boca con boca,
y el corazón contiguo.

Esta noche sé
que no hay mayor bien que la intimidad
ni mayor lujo que el aislamiento.

Por eso quiero que llueva hasta el fin del mundo,
para que nadie nunca deje mi casa.
Hijos, ánclense en mí,
hay tormenta para rato.

# POEMA DEL CHILINDRON

*(para celebrar los diez años de*
*matrimonio tres años después)*

Rosa, éste es el poema
que te debía: cumplo al fin con nuestro cumpleaños.
Recordarás que cenamos en el Málaga, como siempre:
tú: tortilla de papas y cebollas,
salada pero sabrosa (igual que nuestras vidas);
yo: un chilindrón
suculento pero espurio (suple tú la alegoría);
los dos: flan y café
(sabor, y sabiduría).

Así, en ritmo convergente,
hemos soñado los días.
Los dos—más uno, más uno.
Los dos: sabor, y sabiduría.

## LA VIDA ENTERA

¿Y si la vida entera se reduce a esto:
un extravío de juguetes y toallas y la cama sin hacer?
¿Y si mi casa, que fue nido,
se convierte en laberinto?
¿Y si éste resultase ser mi texto definitivo,
mis últimas palabras?

# 3

*Unintelligible Ballads*

# A SENSITIVE MALE'S MEA CULPA

Forgive me, Lord, for this clump between my legs
    that makes me moan and mate.
Forgive the rustle in my loins when Cathy's ass walks by
    or I hold Julia in my arms.
Forgive my glands, my glans, and my gaze.

I confess that my gonads have been up to no good.
My secretions are no secret.
I know that if lust were pubic hair, I'd need a trim.

But then again, Lord, it could be worse.
I haven't raped anyone in weeks.
I molest blondes and redheads exclusively.
I've stayed away from my daughter.
I only fantasize about my niece.
And I am scrupulously upright with Cuban women.

You must know, Lord (you know everything),
you must know how difficult it is
to look Lisa in the eye and not see her pussy.

I wish I were not such a swine.

Oh Lord, please cleanse me,
cast these demons of desire from me.
Let me walk without strutting.
Let me look without leering.
Let me touch without feeling.
I want to fuck without penetration!

Hear my horny cry, sweet Jesus,
take me from the ranks of the rank and the randy
and drop me in a choir of sexless angels.
Mea culpa, mea culpa, mea maxima culpa.

Blessed is he who was born without a hypothalamus.
Blessed is he who does not pay lip service to cunnilingus.
Blessed is he who never drowned in a C-cup.

The Lord is my shepherd,
    I have bunged my last hole.
The Lord is my shepherd,
    I have pierced my last nipple.
The Lord is my shepherd,
    I have trussed up and whipped my last underage virgin.
The Lord is my shepherd,
    My heart and my hard-on
    rejoice in the bosom of the Lord.

## ARS AMANDI

The love of your life is never
the love of your life, anyway.
Either she wasn't to begin with
or (what is less likely) something
goes wrong along the way.
You can grieve and kick and scream about this
or you can take it in stride
—upstroke, downstroke—
cushion the blow as best you can
and swear to one and all
(including your next)
you've never been happier
you've never been more in love.
If she's smart, she'll believe you.

# LEAVE-TAKING TRIO

## I

Middle age is ice age.
When she called you were polite,
you left the room.
I did not speak another word till morning,
but as you were leaving you whispered
that you'd be there if I wanted to talk.
Curt, not courteous, I replied: I won't.

Two days later I got your letter,
and I didn't answer.
You came to my house,
and I didn't open the door.
We passed in the hall,
and I didn't even greet you.
It was nice while it lasted,
but it didn't.
Middle age is ice age, etc.

## II

You leave your American dream
(nightmare in transit)
on a Fourth of July.

She says you're gutless.
You say you're not American.
She says you're a bastard.
You deny it.
She says you've ruined her life.
You say (speaking therapese)
her life's not yours to ruin.
She says you never loved her.
You say I have loved you (pause) good-bye.
She says this is a joke.
You say make it plain good-bye then.

She hangs up.
You follow.
End of another Fourth of July.

III

Write her beauty, write her touch:
the daily details of her limbs
moving past you, her luminous thighs,
her hips astride you, rising and falling.
Write that you will never know this again.

# FED UP (I)

When I get ready to leave,
you will say:
I did not love you enough
I did not fuck you enough
I did not feel you enough.

Look: I loved, fucked, and felt you.
Enough is enough.

## FED UP (II)

When I look into your eyes
I see the twelve tribes of Israel
chasing me.

When I look into your eyes
I see the mohel from Virginia
clipping me.

When I look into your eyes
I see everyone in the family
but me.

When I look into your eyes (so blue)
I see that it's time to stop
looking.

# THE POET DISCUSSES THE OPPOSITE SEX

So what's the difference, you say,
between a cunt and a pussy.

Pussies dream.
Cunts never sleep.

Pussies glow.
Cunts swallow.

Pussies fit.
Cunts you could drive trucks through.

When pussies pee, it's a golden shower.
When cunts pee, you can hear it
all the way to the next block.

A cunt is a lethal weapon of destruction.
Pussies are peace.
(I never met a pussy I didn't like.)

Don't be caught with a cunt in a dark alley
(listen, a cunt *is* a dark alley).

If God had intended women to be cunts,
he'd have given them pricks.

A pussy, by virtue of its pussiness,
is perfection itself.

The universe is a pussy.

# BAD MOUTH

Sensitive—the word gives me the creeps:
a sensitive writer, a sensitive man,
"sensitive stories, full of color and music."

Time to bellow and belch.
Time to reclaim our legacy of foulness:
I stink, therefore I am.
Free to be you and me:
sexist, racist, and homophobic,
not to mention violent: yes!
Born to chop.

Work your wile,
spill your bile,
let it run, run, run, run
into the guts of the sensitive
there to fester and foam.

This is my body,
this is my blood:
eat me.

# GHOST WRITING

I live with ghosts.
Laggard ghosts who wear their fatigue like a sheet
Petulant, unrepentant ghosts who never sleep
Ghosts like mouth sores
Ghosts that look me in the eye at midday
and buzz in my ears in the dead of night
Chinese laundry ghosts
Cuban coffee ghosts
Ghosts that tap and tease and taunt
Politically correct ghosts
Feminist ghosts
Holy ghosts
Ghosts of a chance
Gustavo-come-lately ghosts
Mami and Papi ghosts
The ghosts of all my Nochebuenas past.

My ghosts and I,
we have what you'd call this complicated relationship.
At this very moment, they tap tap tap tap tap
on the back of my head,
just behind my ears.
They know I'm listening, I pretend that I'm not.
But with every ghostly tap my spine vibrates
like a tuning fork.
If I could, I would leap to grab the greatest ghost
of them all and wring his neck like a wet towel.
But my life offers no such satisfactions.
The ghosts extract their pound of flesh
gram by gram, day by day.
You cannot sneeze them away.
They do not respond to treatment or medication
(my therapist is a ghost).

By now, the ghosts are more me than me.
One of them wrote this poem.

## SUNDAY BEAST

Sunday is my day of restlessness.
Though I sit still,
I fuss and fume and fulminate
the length and width of the day.

Who greets me on Sunday
can expect a bark back,
if anything. It's words
like gruff or sullen or surly
or maybe homicidal
that describe my Sunday best,
my Sunday beast.

Come Monday I'm a little hung over
on animosity
but otherwise back to what's normal.
But Sundays I'm a sore sight for anyone's eyes.

Pity the poor jerk
who needs me on a Sunday afternoon.
I'm just as likely to snap
his head off
as I am to pretend
neither one of us is here.
On Sunday I'm bitch, bastard, and baby
all rolled up into one.

(Today is Sunday.)

# QUIET TIME

I seethe, but not too much.
Your careful touch retrieves me.
Nowhere to go but down and in:
many selves to greet there,
where I go.

Where I go: my soul
into our sofa, my head onto your thighs.
I settle, down and in.
Like snow falling, I settle.

What to call this quietness
without peace. What to call it.

What does it mean to settle?
To surrender peak for stability,
but without sinking.
Things that settle: sand or snow.

I seethe, you soothe.
I clamor or clam up: you wait.
Speaking your silence: you wait
for things that settle: sand or snow.

# FOR THE RECORD

To write you a poem
unsure and uncaring
whether you'll find
it years afterwards
and think, was he smart,
wasn't he, was he clever,
wasn't he, wasn't he a wonder.

Not to care except
to have you read it
and think, he loved me.

# JUST ONE WISH

To have looked at you
To have touched you
To have lain beside you
when there was no age
on your body.

# BILINGUAL

In Spanish / en español
las palabras se pegan
al cuerpo y no me veo.
En inglés / in English
las cosas are more equivocal
but your skin is your skin.

# UNPACKING MY LIBRARY

Don't I seem educated to you?
I've already exhibited my Conrad, my Dickens,
my box full of Hemingways.
I showed you how, when I was a freshman in high school,
I scribbled something on my copy of *Paradise Lost*.
Not too many women's novels, I know,
but I do have some Austen, some Didion,
a fair amount of Sontag (and loads of Severo Sarduy).

Where's Wolfe?
I'm sure it's someplace, I reply,
panicking that I may not have any
and not knowing which one you mean.

So what am I trying to prove
to you, who read even Australian novelists
and Margaret Drabble?

I underline books I haven't read
so that when I forget I haven't read them
perhaps I'll think that I have.
You haven't put a line on a margin
in thirty years
(that's quite like you,
unobtrusive even in reading).

But if I finally convince you
that I'm not only smart but cultured,
I'm not sure what that would do to our relationship.

Perhaps it's better this way,
—me trying too hard
—you stringing along
each of us hoodwinking
the other as we place book upon book
neatly on the shelves of our new library.

## SETTLEMENTS

This morning I stopped reading the local paper.
I came back from my rounds feeling relieved
that for once there was no note from my ex,
brewed fresh coffee,
and read the Seawell School News instead.

If I read the paper I can't get settled,
so I've given up current events.
I still have scores to settle but I'm settled.

Tomorrow is Yom Kippur. I'm not fasting.
So this is what settling means.

I'm not sure whether I feel
more settled with the windows in my study
open or shut.
If I open them the pollen sifts through the screens
like hairspray.
If I close them the walls come alive
with hissing ghosts.
Either way it's unsettling.

My conclusion is that being Cuban is unsettling.
I wrote the book that proves it.

Years ago I signed a property settlement.
It didn't settle anything.
But it did teach me the adverbial wisdom
that settling up is not settling down.

But if I can't settle down
I'll settle for settling in,
which may be the most permanent settlement of all.

This morning along with the coffee
I had the three raisin bran muffins

that Mary Anne left for me
in a brown bag on the table.

Somebody loves me.
That settles it. For now.

# OPEN HOUSE

We make love by the window, as usual.
Nothing to hide from the bare trees
and passersby (the trees are more attentive).
Resting, we hear voices.
I think: someone saw us and called the cops,
like that couple in Florida
that a peeping taping Tom captured
in the act at their poolside condo.

No such luck. It's only the movie we rented
clicking on in the next room.
If I want my id on video
I'm going to have to do it myself.

Maybe we should get blinds, Mary Anne says.
No reason, I say,
a month from now it will be spring
and the leaves will cover us,
like Adam and Eve no longer in paradise.

Until then we'll be innocent beasts
in love with our bodies and our selves,
innocent beasts unashamed
and lumbering through this open house,
the only paradise we'll ever need.

# ANNIVERSARY

This is not a minefield, babe,
this is a house.
The two slivers of plaster
I left on top of the vanity
were not a message.
I did not put them
there to say:
Fix it!
It's your fault!
How could you do this to me!

I rushed from the shower
to answer the phone (it was you)
and forgot to dump them
in the wastebasket.
You weren't supposed to see them.

Put down your guard, babe.
Please relax.
The shelling's been over for a year.
The cops haven't knocked on our door in months.
Even my therapist concludes I'm moving
beyond narcissism.
I'm sad, he says, not angry
(he says this is an improvement).

Only fear me you-know-where.
There, one of these days I'm going to grind you
to a quivering pulp,
if you don't do it to me first.
(Gladly me and mine would melt
in your hands, oh dominatrix!)
A little pain never hurt anyone,
but I would never hurt you
unless you asked me to.
(Promises, promises,
you once said.)

I'd be thrilled if the neighbors called the cops
on us for that too.

I love you, babe.
I put down my weapons a while back
and called an end to hostilities
(you knew I wasn't shooting at you anyway).
This quiet's not a truce, babe,
this is peace.

So next time you find
two slivers of plaster, or an empty
shampoo bottle, or my shoes,
think instead: he left them there
because he's mindless,
because I make him happy.

# WITH TIME IN HER HANDS

Mary Anne, from now on
time is your department.
Dates, delays, deferrals, departures
are henceforth your responsibility.

Never again will my tics lead to tocs.
Gone is my temporal lobe, my biological clock, my diary.
I have second-guessed you long enough.
I have two-timed you long enough.
From now on I'm giving you the time of my life.
From now on you alone will spring forward and fall back.
I'm standing still.

Mary Anne, you are now and forever,
mistress of my days,
mistress of my nights,
and of all the time in between.

## PUS AND BOOKS

People send books sometimes
I read them sometimes I don't
(a book on the shelf is worth
two in the hand) books are elastic
they open they close
they clean themselves
they don't say I love you
they always give you one hundred percent.

You know where you are with books
they leave you alone
they have their assigned lovely place
they don't move and they don't tremble
their lifelessness is a wonder.

# TERMS OF ACCOUNT

*Try telling yourself*
*you are not accountable*
*not the life of your tribe*
*the breath of your planet.*
*–Adrienne Rich*

I am not accountable
to the life of my tribe
the breath of my planet.
I am not accountable
to the life of my tribe
the breath of my planet.
I am not accountable
to the life of my tribe
the breath of my planet.
I am not accountable.

# AN AFTERNOON IN JUNE

This is a difficult afternoon
for me, what with Miriam's party
and me not there
to pour Coke, count candles and save children from drowning.

This is a difficult afternoon
for me, the museum's a bore,
the lawn needs mowing
and her pool lies overturned and puddly.

This is a difficult afternoon
for me, suddenly a childless father:
the humming rooms and nothing else.

Ah, but there's snapper
for dinner, and white wine from Australia,
and maybe a movie.
And, like pool season, Miriam always returns.

# DUDE DESCENDING A STAIRCASE

Like a lazy avalanche
he tumbles down the stairs
at seven twenty in the morning.
I know what he's wearing:
white socks,
Umbros down to his knees
under an oversized t-shirt,
a baseball cap pointing backwards
and glasses.

He's a clumpy Michael Jordan
bounding toward adolescence in hightops.
(Vertical leap: two inches—if that.)
As he spills himself on the floor
in front of the TV (today is Saturday),
I turn in bed
to give Mary Anne one last hug.
Feeling the squeeze, she moans
an I-love-you.

By the time I make it out of the room
twenty minutes later,
he's in the kitchen
preparing pancakes.
I'm clear-eyed but woozy.
In the course of this day
he will attend baseball practice,
shoot layups with his tongue hanging out,
accompany me to the tanning salon
and order pizza.

I marvel at this man-boy, my son,
who calls himself machito and tries to strut.
So far so good, I tell myself,
not quite believing it.
In awe of his normalcy,
I wait for something to go awry.

But David doesn't disappoint.
He cans a five-footer and stumbles
on the juke step.
No matter.
Shaqueel's got nothing on him.

As I wipe
the pancake batter from the floor,
I trust that delusion will ripen into sureness.
I trust that reality will settle gently on him.
But for now he's on his way, he is,
my machito in the making
tumbling down the stairs
to a soft, firm landing.

Mary Anne brews the coffee.
Miriam scrambles some eggs like an old hand.
I fry the bacon.
For once everybody eats
everything.
And yes,
the pancakes look terrible
but don't taste half-bad, actually.

# SPLIT ROUTINES

My split routine: I work, and lie in bed,
and have lunch, and lie in bed some more,
and sometimes I masturbate, or I save myself
for gym (or you).
When it was warm I had a yogurt,
vanilla with chocolate chips in a four-ounce cup.

If it's Wednesday, Thursday or Friday
I pick the children up
at school and hear them growl about the spaghetti.
If it's Monday or Tuesday I invent
sweet errands to keep myself in gear.

Today is Thursday, Halloween,
and they're trick-or-treating at their mother's first.
I'll get them at seven
and take them trick-or-treating myself.
After so complete a Halloweening
they will end up with two stashes of fruit and candy
(joint custody spoils).

Such double lives they lead!
Even their hearts must be cleft in two.

A while back Miriam used to wake up
in the middle of the night and wonder which house
she was in. When she cried she wondered
whose arms were around her. And when she unstuck her eyes
in the morning she had to guess
whose lips would greet her sleepy stare.

She has two blankets, two pillows, two turtles,
and two toothbrushes: think of that!
My kids must have their own split
routines to keep themselves in gear.

But maybe running all these double tracks
will serve them later. Maybe

it will make them sturdy, make them subtle,
teach them to live with ambiguity.

For these kids already know
what it took me forty years to learn:
there's always another toothbrush,
another blanket, another bed.

# LOVE AT LAST RESORT

Knowing that you are moved
not by tears or terror,
I sift through the details
and brace for the detonations.

A bomb goes off behind my back.
I'm rattled, and grow a little deafer.
No, darling, you say, please don't shake,
you're not a leaf in autumn.

You're still soothing
when another bomb explodes at my feet.
No, darling, you say, don't quiver,
the earth's not really moving.

By now I can barely hear you
and the bombs keep on exploding.
Crackling like a twig in the fire,
I'm feeling more and more precarious.
Still you soothe:
No, darling, you say, don't give up now,
please don't give up now,
now that the war's almost over.

And as you say this, you
put your arms around me
and slip something smooth
and small into my pocket.

# THE OPERATION

It had the size of a small egg
and the look perhaps of a testicle in its sac.
It was removed yesterday morning.

The cyst had nested on my back for years,
cradled halfway between my lungs,
growing from a ripple on the skin
to the ripe red pouch I beheld
when it was no longer my body.

I record this with some sadness.
I had become attached to my cyst
(and my cyst to me).
I knew my cyst was as close as I'd ever come
to being pregnant.

And now it was over.
The operation lasted maybe fifteen minutes
and nothing hurt except the needle.
Linda the nurse held my hand.
I took it like a man.

# A CHANGE OF SKIN

I am asleep. I am dreaming about my foreskin, which is
growing back. Like a lizard's tail, it's growing back. The mohel
(I guess that's who he is) explains to Rosa (I guess that's who
she is) that, in order to prevent new growth, a retractor should
have been placed on my penis. After the bris they should've
stretched me out, tied me down, and left the clamp there for a
couple of days. Give the snip time to take. But since this wasn't
done, my foreskin is growing back luxuriantly. Growing back
with gusto. Growing back with Gustavo. Growing back with a
goyische vengeance. The more they clip, the faster it grows.
Soon I have to give up jockeys for boxers. I have to stop going
to gym. It takes me hours to clean myself. Smegma becomes a
household word. I look in the dictionary for synonyms:
prepuce. My foreskin gets so long and baggy that it only fits
inside my pants if I coil it. Even then the bulge is unmistakable,
but I'm not embarrassed. I remember the bullfighters who
used to stuff their suit of lights with hankies. Then the alarm
goes off. I wake up with an erection and I look down at my
foreskin, which no mohel has ever touched.

# DEATH IS ALWAYS PLURAL

Death is always plural, he said.
Who dies takes himself plus
those we knew through him.
Who dies multiplies absence
by the number of names no one will hear again.
Who dies pockets multitudes in his casket,
sequesters crowds under his shroud.

So compound your sorrow, he says,
factor your grief, think big.
It takes all the pain you can muster
to mourn the unsuspecting dead.

# LAST WORDS

Grunt and gasp:
losing it
losing it
having lost it, lost it once and again
and for all, already,
grunt and gasp.

Your last words better than words
your last breath deeper than life
leaving me leaving you
speechless once and again
and for always, already
Say it all: grunt and gasp.

## DEAD STOP

I just want to stop,
cease and desist. For once:
wheels no longer spinning
brain no longer churning
neurons no longer firing
nerves no longer crackling
heart no longer racing
muscles no longer twitching
groin no longer tingling.

It's not dying I'm talking about,
understand me.
I love my little life (in general).
What I want is to come to a dead stop
but without dying.
I want to be at rest, resting, resisting
the least movement of mind or muscle.

# ON WHETHER MY FATHER DESERVES A POEM

I will never say
my father used to say.
My father never said
anything
(except dirty jokes
with each phone call).
Scratch idea for poem
with father's words.

My father did not teach
by example.
My father never acted
decisively
(he waffled and gambled
and lost).
So scratch idea for poem
with father's deeds.

Absent words and deeds
what's left me of my father
to write this orphan poem?

# EVITA Y GUSTAVITO (COMPOSITE)

Little Eva believes life is a jumble
   —thinks sex is overrated
   —prefers the company of horses (they don't dissemble)
   —rags on Hemingway
   —feels the magic of the redwoods
   and lusts for lines.

Little Gustavo likes his life simple
   —likes his sex transcendent (who doesn't)
   —cares less for horses, redwoods, or Hemingway
   and will give you all the lines
   provided he can keep the words to himself.

Evita y Gustavito met at Mike's funeral,
went to dinner, shared Latin kisses,
sipped Jamaican rhum, and smooched
at the corner of Commodore and Grand.
(She said—Am I supposed to remember this?)

He grabbed her ass (wow), she took him home.
(Little Eva is a cautious sort.)
Still, he cannot forget the feel of her hand on his hair
and she'll doubtless remember _____ .

(fill-in the blank and finish the poem:
Gustavo is cautious too).

# THE POET'S MOTHER GIVES HIM
# A BIRTHDAY PRESENT

Thirty masses is what I got
for my birthday. Thirty masses
and a bottle of Paco Rabanne.

> *Gustavo Pérez Firmat*
> *will share in the following*
> *spiritual benefits for one year:*
> *Thirty Masses*
> *Two Novenas of Masses*
> *Requested by Mrs. Gustavo Pérez*
> *Signed: Father Edward.*
> *Salesian Missions.*

It must be I'm tottering on the brink.
It must be I'm high on the road to perdition.
I must be losing my soul.
Surely these are critical masses.

Jump start my soul, Ma.
Pile mass on mass till I stop fibrillating.
Drip cool hosannas into the IV.
Pump me with 42 cc's of saintliness,
one for each of my errant years.
Slip that catholic catheter into my pipi
and bring my peccant prostate to its knees.
Have me break out in ejaculations, Ma.

Do it, Ma.
Make me holy.
Put an end to this wanton life.
I shall sin no more.
And all for you, Ma.
All for you.

*May the joy of this your birthday*
*Continue all year through*
*And make each day that comes your way*
*A happy day for you!*

# LIME CURE

I'm filling my house with limes
to keep away the evil spirits.
I'm filling my house with limes
to help me cope.
I have limes on the counters, under the sink,
inside the washbasin.
My refrigerator is stuffed with limes
(there's no longer any space for meat and potatoes).
Faking onionship, they hang from the walls.
Like golf balls, they have the run of the carpet
(but I would not drive them away).

I stash them in flowerpots.
I put them on bookshelves.
I keep them on my desk, cuddling with my computer.
I have two limes in every drawer of every chest
of every room.
I don't bathe, I marinade.

At night, I think of their cores, plump and wet.
I imagine myself taking off the peel and squeezing
until they burst in my hands.
I taste the tart juice dripping on my tongue.
I shudder.
Then I sleep peacefully inside green dreams of lime
and when I wake, I bask in the morning's lime light.

Were it not for limes, I would not know
what to do with myself.
I could not bear this loneliness.
I would burst.
But there is a wisdom in limes, an uneventfulness
that soothes my seething and whispers to me:
think, be still, and think some more,
and when the night arrives, dream of juice.

# WHAT'S WRONG WITH ME

I pick my nose.
I'm shallow.
I spend too much time on my ties.
I get melancholy (baby).
When I come, I don't come cheap.
You can't trust me with matches.
My stomach gives me away.
I wasn't born in Kansas.
I keep my hands to myself.
I pay my debts.
I tremble.

**Acknowledgments** (continued)

Some of the poems included here originally appeared in the following publications:

*The Bilingual Review:* "The Southern Part of Heaven," "Bloomington, Illinois," "Poema de amor al general Sandino," Vol. 7, No. 3 (1980); "Carolina Cuban," "Home," Vol. 9, No. 2 (1982); "Seeing Snow," "Before I Was a Writer," Vol. 11, No. 3 (1984); "The Operation," "The Poet Discusses the Opposite Sex," "Ars Amandi," Vol. 17, No. 1 (1992).

*Linden Lane Magazine:* "Waiting Game," Vol. 1, No. 2 (1983); "Romance de Coral Gables," "Día de los padres en Chapel Hill," Vol. 3, No. 2 (1984); "A mi hermano el impostor," Vol. 4, No. 2 (1985); "A Likely Story," Vol. 8, No. 1 (1989); "De última hora," Vol. 10, No. 1 (1991); "Dude Descending a Staircase," Vol. 12, No. 1 (1993); "Leave-Taking Trio," Vol. 12, No. 1 (1993).

*Mariel:* "Mínima elegía bilingüe," "Provocaciones," Vol. 1, No. 3 (1983).

*Término Magazine:* "Carnet de identidad," Vol. 2, No. 8 (1984).

*Caribbean Review:* "Turning the Times Tables," Vol. 15, No. 3 (1987).

*Miami Mensual:* "Filosofías del no," Vol. 9, No. 10 (1989).

*Latino Stuff Review:* "Plantado," "Nobody Knows My Name," No. 2 (1990); "Tres poemas martianos," No. 3 (1991); "A Sensitive Male's Mea Culpa," No. 9 (1992).